Contents

What is living? 4

Plants 6

What is non-living? 8

Moving 10

Senses 12

Eating and drinking 14

Finding food 16

Breathing 18

Getting rid of waste 20

New life 22

Living things die 24

Things that were alive 26

Living or non-living? 28

Glossary 30

Answers 31

Index 32

Any words appearing in the text in bold, **like this**, are explained in the Glossary.

What is living?

This cat is living. You can tell that the
cat is alive because it is licking its paw.
If there is a loud noise, it will jump.

LIVING AND NON-LIVING

Angela Royston

Heinemann
LIBRARY

www.heinemann.co.uk/library
Visit our website to find out more information about **Heinemann Library** books.

To order:
☎ Phone 44 (0) 1865 888066
🖹 Send a fax to 44 (0) 1865 314091
💻 Visit the Heinemann Bookshop at www.heinemann.co.uk/library to browse our
  catalogue and order online.

First published in Great Britain by Heinemann
Library, Halley Court, Jordan Hill, Oxford
OX2 8EJ, part of Harcourt Education.

Heinemann is a registered trademark of Harcourt
Education Ltd.

© Harcourt Education Ltd 2003
First published in paperback in 2004
The moral right of the proprietor has been
asserted.

Editorial: Andrew Farrow and Dan Nunn
Design: Jo Hinton-Malivoire and
  Tinstar Design Limited (www.tinstar.co.uk)
Picture Research: Maria Joannou and Sally Smith
Production: Viv Hichens

Originated by Blenheim Colour Ltd
Printed and bound in China by
  South China Printing Company

ISBN 0 431 13724 2 (hardback)
07 06 05 04 03
10 9 8 7 6 5 4 3 2 1

ISBN 0 431 13730 7 (paperback)
08 07 06 05 04
10 9 8 7 6 5 4 3 2 1

**British Library Cataloguing
in Publication Data**
Royston, Angela
Living and non-living. – (My world of science)
1. Life – Juvenile literature
2. Life sciences – Juvenile literature
I. Title
570

A full catalogue record for this book is available
from the British Library.

Acknowledgements
The publishers would like to thank the following
for permission to reproduce photographs:
Bruce Coleman Collection pp. **5**, **22**; Chris
Honeywell pp. **15**, **26**; David C. Tomlinson p. **13**;
Digital Vision pp. **10**, **19**, **25**; Getty Images p. **18**;
KPT Power Photos p. **11**; NHPA p. **24**; Photodisc
p.**7**; Pictor International p. **20**; Powerstock Zefa
pp. **4**, **16**; Robert Harding Picture Library pp. **12**,
17; Trevor Clifford pp. **8**, **9**, **14**, **23**, **27**, **29**;
Trip pp. **21** (H. Rogers), **28** (G. Contorakes);
Wildlife Matters p. **6**.

Cover photograph reproduced with permission of
Rex Features.

Every effort has been made to contact copyright
holders of any material reproduced in this book.
Any omissions will be rectified in subsequent
printings if notice is given to the publishers.

All animals are living things. Humans are a kind of animal, too. How many different kinds of animal can you see in this picture? (Answer on page 31.)

Plants

These plants are alive. You can tell
they are alive because they have
green leaves and grow. Each plant
grows from a tiny **seed**.

Plants grow taller and taller. Trees go on growing for many years. Each year they grow new twigs and flowers, and new green leaves, too.

What is non-living?

None of the things in this picture are living. They cannot move on their own. They only move if they are pushed.

This doll cannot move and she does not grow. She is said to be non-living. Non-living things stay the same unless something else changes them.

Moving

These zebras are galloping over the land. Living things can move by themselves. Most animals have legs, wings or **fins**. They use them to move.

Non-living things cannot move on their own. A car or truck can move very fast, but a person has to start the **engine** and then drive it.

Senses

Animals and people can see, hear, feel, smell and taste. This is how they know what is going on around them. Seeing, hearing, feeling, smelling and tasting are called **senses**.

Plants have different senses. Their senses allow them to react to the world around them. A sunflower grows upwards. The flower turns so that it always points towards the Sun.

Eating and drinking

Living things need to eat food and drink water to stay alive. What is in the sandwich that this boy is eating? (Answer on page 31.)

Plants use their leaves to make their own food. They drink in water through their **roots**. Plants die if they do not get enough water.

Finding food

This **cheetah** is hunting an **antelope**. Some animals, like the cheetah, eat only meat. Others, like the antelope, eat only plants.

Non-living things do not eat and drink.
This lion is carved out of stone and so
is non-living. Even if you put food in its
mouth, it could not eat it!

Breathing

Living things need to take in **oxygen**. Oxygen is a kind of gas. This boy is **breathing in** oxygen from the air. The fish breath in oxygen from the water.

The snail and the plants are taking in oxygen too. But the rock is not breathing, because non-living things do not need oxygen.

Getting rid of waste

All living things produce waste. The brown cowpats are waste that has been produced by the two cows. **Urine** (pee) is also a way of getting rid of waste.

This statue is covered with waste. The statue does not produce waste, because it is not alive. Which animals have produced this waste? (Answer on page 31.)

New life

Living things produce babies or **seeds** that will become like themselves. These puppies will grow up to be adult dogs like their mother and father.

If these seeds are planted, they will grow into new plants. But spoons and other non-living things cannot make copies of themselves. This is because they are non-living.

Living things die

Many flowers and **insects** live only
for a few months. Then they die.
After they have died, they slowly
rot away.

Other living things live for many years. This giant tortoise could live for 100 years before it becomes very old and dies.

Things that were alive

These things are made of wood. Wood comes from trees that were once alive. Wool, paper and cotton also come from things that were once alive.

Things that were once alive have to be **treated** to stop them **rotting**. Non-living things do not need to be treated. These toys can last for a very long time.

Living or non-living?

This photo shows some things that are living. They include the children, the puppies and the flowers. Which things are non-living? (Answer on page 31.)

The table, the chair and the door
are non-living. But there are also
four living things in this room. What
are they? (Answer on page 31.)

Glossary

antelope an animal that looks like a deer. Antelopes live in Africa and Asia.

breathe in pull air or oxygen into the body

cheetah a big cat that hunts antelopes and other animals for its food. Cheetahs live in Africa and Asia.

engine a machine that makes something move

fins flat parts of the body of fish and other water animals. The animals use their fins to steer.

gas a gas has no shape. It spreads out through the air.

insect small animal with six legs and antennae. Bees, flies, ladybirds and beetles are all insects.

oxygen a kind of gas that all living things need to breathe

roots the parts of a plant that are below ground

rot slowly break up into little pieces

seed part of a plant that grows into a new plant

senses the ways in which a living thing finds out about what is around it. Seeing and feeling are senses.

treat to protect something using special chemicals

urine liquid that animals make to get rid of unwanted water

Answers

page 5
There are two different kinds of animal.
These are an elephant and some people.

page 14
The sandwich contains lettuce, cheese,
tomato, ham and cucumber.

page 21
The birds have produced the waste on
the statue.

page 28
The fence, the basket and the children's
clothes are non-living.

page 29
The girl, the dog and the two plants
are living.

Index

animals 4–5, 10, 12, 16, 22, 25, 28–29
breathing 18–19
death 24–25
drinking 15
eating 14, 16
materials 26–27
moving 10–11
non-living things 8–9, 11, 17, 23, 28–29
oxygen 18–19
people 5, 28–29
plants 6–7, 13, 15, 24, 29
puppies 22
seeds 23
senses 12–13
waste 20–21